CCSS **Genre** Nonfiction

M000093471

Essential Question
How do animals help each other?

Penguins All Around

by Donna Loughran

Chapter 1

Meet the Penguins

Penguins live in large groups.

Penguins are birds, but they cannot fly. When penguins walk on their little feet, they **waddle** from side to side. They can hop and slide, too. Penguins are fun to watch!

Penguins are very good swimmers! They have small wings that help them paddle through the water. **Webbed** feet help them swim, too. If you watch penguins swim, it looks like they're flying underwater.

Chapter 2
How Do Penguins Live?

Penguins are good divers.

Did you know that penguins are good divers? They can **dive** deep into the sea to look for food. Penguins can stay under the water for several minutes at a time.

krill

Penguins feed together. They eat fish and **krill**. Krill, which are small shrimp, are easy to find because they float on the water. If penguins want to eat fish, they must dive deeper!

Seals hunt penguins for food.

Have you ever heard someone say there's safety in numbers? That's one reason that penguins live in groups. Another thing that protects penguins from danger is the color of their feathers. Because they have white feathers on their bellies, they can blend in with the snow. Black feathers help them hide in the sea.

Swimming penguins are hard to see from above.

Some penguins live in icy cold places. These smart penguins huddle together to **shield** each other from the cold temperatures. After standing on the outside of the group for awhile, they move to the center. That's where they can warm up!

Penguins in the huddle shift about every minute so everyone gets a turn inside.

Chapter 3
Penguin Chicks

This penguin rests in a grass nest.

Each year, penguins make a nest with a partner. They are getting the nest ready to hold an egg! Some penguin pairs use stones to make a nest. Other penguins make a hole that they fill with grass.

Look closely. Do you see the egg? Mom and Dad will keep the egg warm. Some dads keep an egg warm by holding it between their feet and belly.

When will the egg crack open? You'll have to wait and see!

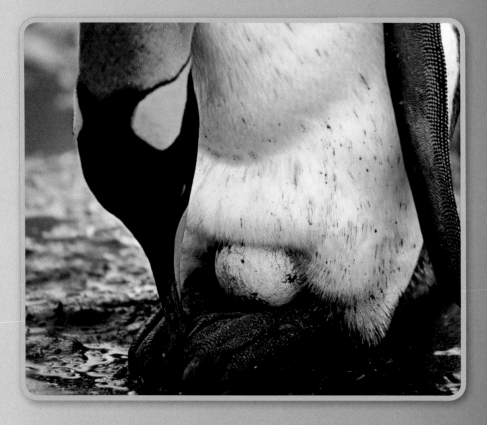

The flap of skin that warms the egg is called a brood flap.

The baby chicks have hatched! At first, the chicks don't look like Mom or Dad. But, soon they will. Mom and Dad work as a team to care for the babies. When hungry chicks call, Mom and Dad bring them food.

The baby penguins get bigger and bigger! Soon they will go out to the open sea. Look how the blue sea sparkles! The penguins will stay at sea until it is time to build new nests.

These chicks have fluffy gray feathers.

Respond to Reading

Retell

Use your own words to retell important details in *Penguins All Around.*

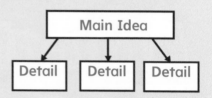

Text Evidence

1. How do penguins get their food?
   Main Idea and Key Details

2. How do penguins keep safe from danger? Main Idea and Key Details

3. Is *Penguins All Around* fiction or nonfiction? How can you tell? Genre

Compare Texts
Read about how animals work together.

Animals Work Together!

Elephants live in groups in the wild. They work together to keep each other safe and to care for the young.

Dolphins live and look for food in groups called pods. This helps dolphins stay safe from the danger of sharks.

Dolphins usually swim at speeds of about 7 miles per hour.

Ants live in groups called colonies.

Ants live in large groups. They help each other build nests. They work together to look for food, too.

Make Connections

Look at both stories. How are penguins like the animals you read about here? Text to Text

Glossary

dive *(DIGHV)* to drop or leap into water *(page 4)*

krill *(KRIL)* a small, shrimp-like sea animal *(page 5)*

shield *(SHEELD)* to protect *(page 7)*

waddle *(WAH-duhl)* to walk in short steps by moving from side to side *(page 2)*

webbed *(WEBD)* having skin that connects the toes on a foot *(page 3)*

Index

Focus on
Science

Purpose To compare two animals

What to Do

Step 1 ▶ Pick two animals that you read about.

Step 2 ▶ Draw a chart like the one below.

Alike	Different

Step 3 ▶ Write two ways the animals you chose are alike. Write two ways they are different.

Conclusion Share what you learned with the class.